Primo dizionario illustrato
Animali

First Picture Dictionary
Animals

Farfalla
Butterfly

Maiale
Pig

Volpe
Fox

Coniglio
Rabbit

Illustrato da Anna Ivanir

www.kidkiddos.com
Copyright ©2025 by KidKiddos Books Ltd.
support@kidkiddos.com

All rights reserved. No part of this book may be reproduced in any form or by any electronic or mechanical means, including information storage and retrieval systems, without written permission from the publisher, except in the case of a reviewer, who may quote brief passages embodied in critical articles or in a review.
First edition, 2025

Library and Archives Canada Cataloguing in Publication
First Picture Dictionary – Animals (Italian English Bilingual edition)
ISBN: 978-1-83416-291-1 paperback
ISBN: 978-1-83416-292-8 hardcover
ISBN: 978-1-83416-290-4 eBook

Animali selvatici
Wild Animals

Tigre
Tiger

Elefante
Elephant

Leone
Lion

Giraffa
Giraffe

✦ *La giraffa è l'animale terrestre più alto.*
✦ *A giraffe is the tallest animal on land.*

Scimmia
Monkey

Animali selvatici
Wild Animals

Ippopotamo
Hippopotamus

Panda
Panda

Volpe
Fox

Rinoceronte
Rhino

Cervo
Deer

Alce
Moose

Lupo
Wolf

✦ *L'alce è un ottimo nuotatore e può immergersi per mangiare piante!*
✦ A moose is a great swimmer and can dive underwater to eat plants!

Scoiattolo
Squirrel

Koala
Koala

✦ *Lo scoiattolo nasconde le noci per l'inverno, ma a volte dimentica dove le ha messe!*
✦ A squirrel hides nuts for winter, but sometimes forgets where it put them!

Gorilla
Gorilla

Animali domestici
Pets

Canarino
Canary

✦ *La rana può respirare sia attraverso la pelle che con i polmoni!*
✦ *A frog can breathe through its skin as well as its lungs!*

Porcellino d'India
Guinea Pig

Rana
Frog

Criceto
Hamster

Pesce rosso
Goldfish

Cane
Dog

✦Alcuni pappagalli possono imitare le parole e perfino ridere come un essere umano!

✦Some parrots can copy words and even laugh like a human!

Gatto
Cat

Pappagallo
Parrot

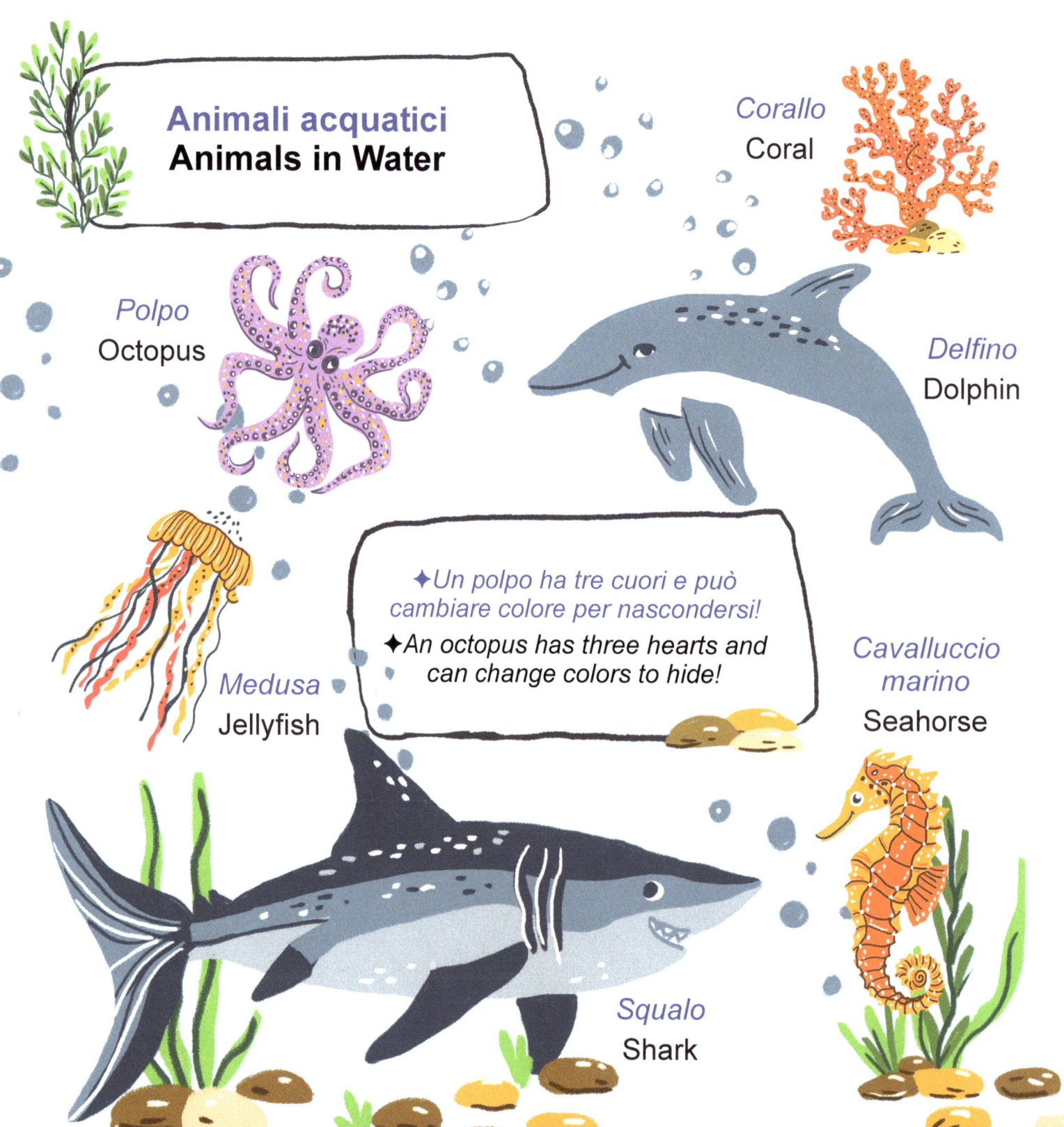

Tasso
Badger

Istrice
Porcupine

Marmotta
Groundhog

✦ *La lucertola può far ricrescere la coda se la perde!*
✦ A lizard can grow a new tail if it loses one!

Lucertola
Lizard

Formica
Ant

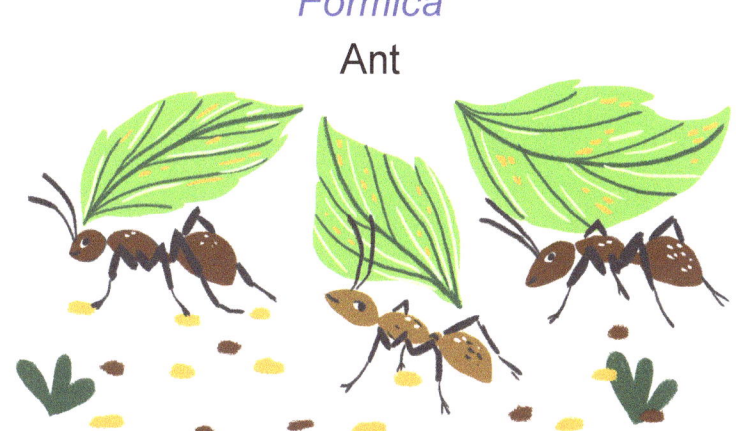

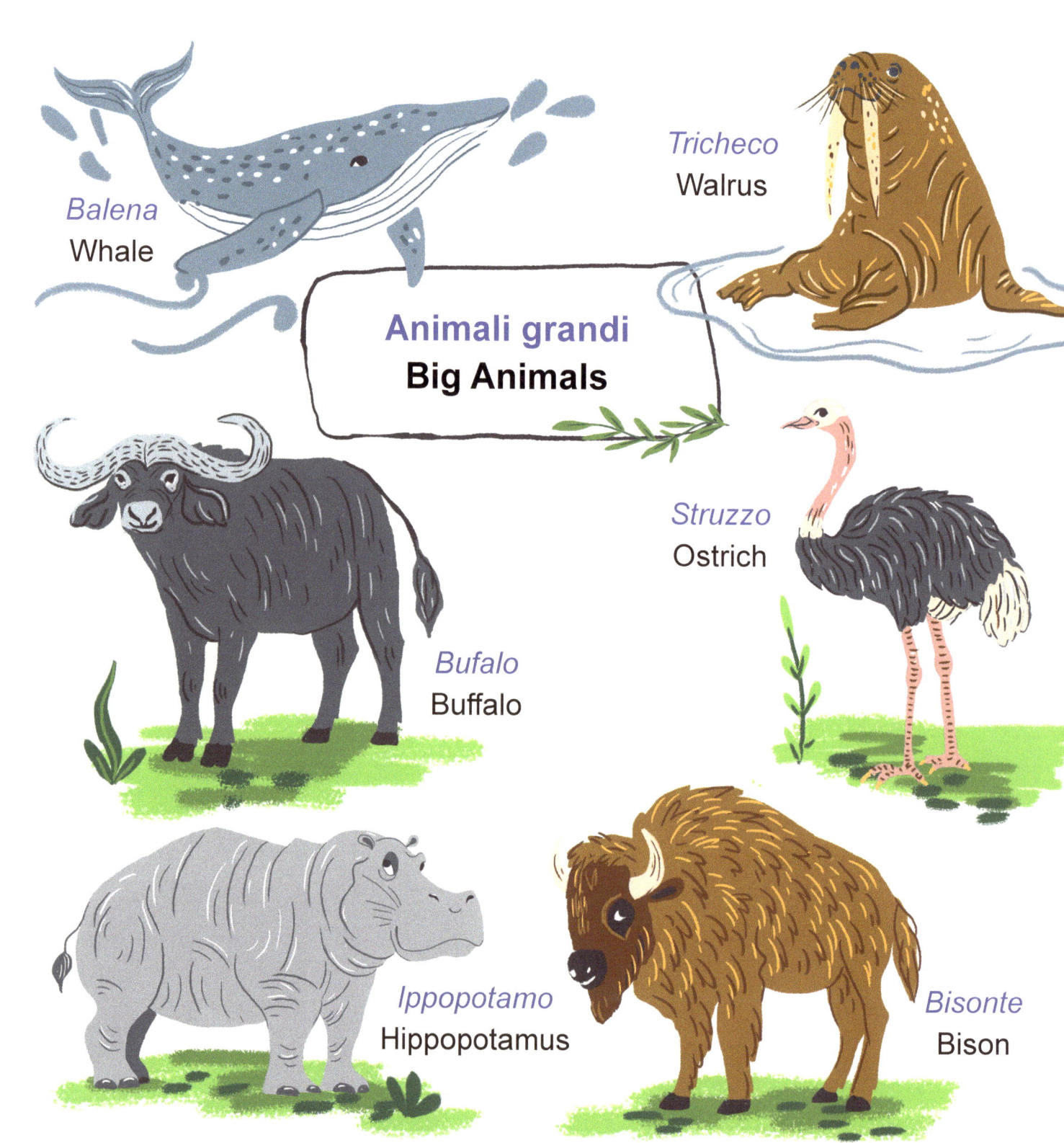

Animali piccoli
Small Animals

Camaleonte
Chameleon

Ragno
Spider

✦ *Lo struzzo è l'uccello più grande, ma non può volare!*
✦ An ostrich is the biggest bird, but it cannot fly!

Ape
Bee

✦ *La lumaca porta la sua casa sulla schiena e si muove molto lentamente.*
✦ A snail carries its home on its back and moves very slowly.

Lumaca
Snail

Topo
Mouse

Gufo
Owl

Pipistrello
Bat

✦ *Il gufo caccia di notte e usa il suo udito per trovare il cibo!*
✦ An owl hunts at night and uses its hearing to find food!

✦ *La lucciola si illumina di notte per trovare altre lucciole.*
✦ A firefly glows at night to find other fireflies.

Procione
Raccoon

Tarantola
Tarantula

Animali colorati
Colorful Animals

Il fenicottero è rosa
A flamingo is pink

Il gufo è marrone
An owl is brown

Il cigno è bianco
A swan is white

Il polpo è viola
An octopus is purple

La rana è verde
A frog is green

- *La rana è verde, così può nascondersi tra le foglie.*
- A frog is green, so it can hide among the leaves.

L'orso polare è bianco
A polar bear is white

La volpe è arancione
A fox is orange

Il koala è grigio
A koala is grey

La pantera è nera
A panther is black

Il pulcino è giallo
A chick is yellow

Animali e i loro piccoli
Animals and Their Babies

Mucca e Vitello
Cow and Calf

Gatto e Gattino
Cat and Kitten

Gallina e Pulcino
Chicken and Chick

✦ *Il pulcino parla con sua madre ancora prima di nascere*
✦ A chick talks to its mother even before it hatches.

Cane e Cucciolo
Dog and Puppy

www.ingramcontent.com/pod-product-compliance
Lightning Source LLC
LaVergne TN
LVHW072004060526
838200LV00010B/276